NONZEN POEMS

BOOKS AND CHAPBOOKS BY MORGAN GIBSON

POETRY

Our Bedroom's Underground, with Barbara Gibson
Mayors of Marble
Stones Glow Like Lovers' Eyes
Dark Summer
Wakeup
Speaking of Light
Kokoro: Heart-Mind, with Keiko Matsui Gibson
The Great Brook Book
Nonzen Poems

PROSE

Kenneth Rexroth
Revolutionary Rexroth: Poet of East-West Wisdom
Among Buddhas in Japan
Tantric Poetry of Kūkai (Kōbō Daishi) Japan's Buddhist Saint,
with Hiroshi Murakami

NONZEN POEMS

BY

Morgan Gibson

Printed Matter Press
Tokyo

NONZEN POEMS

Edited, laid out, and designed by Joe Zanghi
Editor of Printed Matter Press
Cover designed and laid out by Akemi Shinohara

Order individual copies in the USA from
Morgan Gibson (North Hollywood CA)
E-mail: nonzenpoet@mac.com

Order copies worldwide from:
Printed Matter Press
Z Bldg. 2F,
2-8-14 Kitaueno, Taito-ku,
Tokyo, Japan 110-0014
E-mail: info@printedmatterpress.com
http://www.printedmatterpress.com

First edition

Printed in Japan

ISBN 978-193360622-4

Dedicated to my inspiring children

Julia, Lucy, and Christopher Sō Gibson (Matsui Sō)

ACKNOWLEDGMENTS

I am grateful to Joe Zanghi of Printed Matter Press for laying out and publishing this book, Akemi Shinohara for designing and laying out the cover, Robert Bly, Leza Lowitz, antler, and the late Elizabeth Gray Vining for their kind blurbs, and the following editors and curators for posting my work online for many years: Karl Young (Kenosha WI) at *Light & Dust Anthology of Poetry* (http://www.thing.net/~grist/l&d/lighthom.htm; Ken Knabb at *Bureau of Public Secrets* http://www.bopsecrets.org (Berkeley CA); August Highland (San Diego CA) at *Muse Apprentice Guild* (discontinued); and Chris Bazzett at *Joyful Noise Daycare* (Traverse City MI) http://www.joyfulnoisedaycare/com/morganpoems.pdf

I am especially grateful to Hen House Studios for permission to use above "About the Poet" the frame/photo of me from Lindsay D. Mofford's video of *The Signature of All Things*, a documentary on Kenneth Rexroth filmed at Beyond Baroque Poetry Center in Venice CA on December 5, 2005.

I am also grateful to Vickie Burton and the late Ed Burton for including some of these poems in three of my books and several broadsides published by their Morgan Press in Milwaukee WI ("Morgan" is coincidental); to Thomas Montag for issuing a broadside of my "Crystal Sunlake" and other poems in *Sorts* published by his Monday Morning Press (Milwaukee WI); and to David Carr at Four Zoas Night House for publishing two editions of *The Great Brook Book* (hard and soft) and *Wakeup* (Boston MA).

I also thank editors, publishers, and authors for including some of my poems in the following books and chapbooks by others: Taylor Mignon's *Poets Carrying the Rexroth Flame* (Tokyo); Geoffrey Gardner's *For Rexroth* (NYC): The Ark; Martin J. Rosenblum's *Brewing: 20 Milwaukee Poets:* Giligia Press (Lyme Center NH); Sherry Reniker's *Edge; International Arts Interface* and *World's Edge* anthology (Kawasaki Japan); *Fine Frenzy*; Richard Grossinger and Lindy Hough's *Io; Vermont* (Plainfield VT): North American Books; *The Literary Review; Poems Out of Wisconsin, New Poetry Out of Wisconsin*, and *Wisconsin History in Poetry;* Hillel Wright's *Off Beat* (on Allen Ginsberg), Printed Matter Press (Tokyo); *Truck* and *Truck Vermont Anthology* (VT).

I also thank editors of the following American periodicals for publishing some of my poems: *Amalgamated Holding Company; American Haiku; Antioch Review; Arion's Dolphin; Arts in Society; Beloit Poetry Journal; Berkeley Barb; Bugle-American; Choice; Coastlines; cold-drill; Confrontation; Contact II; Crosscurrents; December; Die Young; Experiment; Exquisite Corpse; Farmer's Market; Four Zoas; Gam; Green Mountains Review; Hammers; Hiroshima Shadows; Hummingbird; Image; Kaleidoscope; Massachusetts Review; Measure; Mikromegas; New Mexico Quarterly; Nexus; Noctiluca; North American Review; Our Way; Poetry Now; Poetry Society of America Bulletin; Prairie Schooner; Roots Forming;* Angela Peckinpaugh's *Sackbut Review;* Jake Leed's *Shellys; Sorts;* Uri Hertz's *Third Rail; University Review; Wild Earth; Wisconsin Review,* and especially *Chicago Review* for publishing some of my long "I-Thou Poem for Kenneth Rexroth's Centenary" in its *Rexroth Issue* 52:2/3/4 (Autumn 2006) 236, and online at www.britannica.com/bps and the whole poem at http://humanities.uchicago.edu/orgs/review/index_52_2_3_4.shtml

Thanks also to these editors and publishers in Japan: *Abiko Quarterly; Ao; Blue Canyon; Blue Jacket; Bohemian; Hiroshima Signpost;* Richard Evanoff's *Japan Environment Monitor; Ko-e;* Yuzuru Katagiri's *Kyoto Review;* John Einarsen's *Kyoto Journal; Michi;* John Solt's *One Mind; Poetry Tokyo: Sei-en; Sakura; The Plaza;* Sherry Reniker's *World's Edge;* Suzanne Kamata's *Yomimono,* and *Printed Matter* magazine and anthologies: *Faces in the Crowd, Poesie Yaponesia,* and *Jungle Crows;* and Scott Watson's *Bongos of the Lord.*

Also: Canada: *Descant.* UK: *The Little Word Machine; Prism* and *Prism Anthology; Outposts.* India: *Poet;* Switzerland: *Poesie Vivante;* Italy: *Prospetti.*

CONTENTS

PART I — ONE BREATH POEMS

PART II — BREATHING, SWIMMING, SNOWING

PART III — SHADOWS OF BUDDHALAND

PART I

ONE BREATH POEMS

IN MUMMY-BAG

In mummy-bag
in a tomb of leaves
I gasp for you.

*

Here, love secrets
in my bones:
too long.

*

I lost all
friends but you.
Now you.

*

Snow fools
with yellowing leaves
as you fooled me.

*

Thunder growls over
the mountains.
I gasp for you to return.

*

Ghosts blow
from tamaracks
yellowing in snow.

*

Land of
loess and
loss.

*

The Buddha
stares at headlights
in the rain.

*

Overheated
hungry for you
I try to write off love.

*

Like you
the sky
shuts me out.

*

Snow chokes
and blinds me
in pursuit.

*

Watching snow
listening to snow
and "snow."

*

Sounding
shaping
darkness.

SNOW GLARE OF ABSENCE

The snow
glare of
absence
under
the moon.

*

Moonlit falling snow
shapes faces flying
past, forever lost.

*

Snow breathing on snow.
Deer are bleeding in snow
that drifts behind the summer-house.

*

Washing my face in snow
in the middle of the night
my heart still beating

half my life behind me
half before me
living half a life.

*

Under the December moon
I broke off a twig of pine
and a twig of Washington Hawthorne
with wrinkled orange berries.

Inside I planted the twigs
in a cup filled with
Japanese stones.

The needles were dusty cold.
Among them berries glowed
like distant villages burning.

*

The snow
holds the dead
together:

the whole
world is one
cold eye.

*

Birds before dawn
singing
together.

I am ready
to let
go.

Listen as if
when they stop
we die.

*

Is the snow
too bright
for form?

Shining
surrounds me
absorbs me.

Where

did

I

go?

DARK WINDOW TO THE WORLD

Who stares at
me?

Who?
me?

*

Whose
blank eyes
open mine?

*

Whose
mute lips
echo?

*

Whose
frown webs
the window?

*

Whose
head floats
in the night?

*

Whose
hands lie caged
on the page?

*

Whose
hands join
in depths?

*

Who
sounds
the void?

O window window
window:
open to the wind!

*

The wind in the wind-
ow wastes its breath on
a night of nobody.

*

I waste my breath on
nobody while the wind
mixes up my mind.

*

Wind
in leaves
in the dark
I am still.

*

In the dark wind
I forgot I stood
in the dark wind.

*

Wanting
the wind
that wants.

*

Wind on my face.
Hair rises
I rise
and fall.

*

Wind
touches my cheeks
like a woman
forgotten

*

You?
From another
world?

*

Are you
forgetting
I remember you?

*

What do we know
of you
or me?

*

Wind
in the woods
where are you?

*

Wind
a-
way.

*

Listening
where the wind
was.

*

Fly
in web of window
I?

*

I
buzz and
die.

*

Webbed
in the window
to the world.

*

Who
hears my buzz
as anyone's?

*

Who's moved?
Who buzzes
back?

*

Whose
words rip webs
off the world?

*

Where am I?
In world or
word?

*

In world
I'm webbed.
In words
I fly.

*

Darkly
webbed
in world.

*

Bright
words
fly.

*

Words
know no
world.

*

And I?
In light
or dark?

*

Sickening
in the dark world
till the bright word.

*

The air
waits
to be breathed.

*

A breath.
A poem.

*

Sink-
ing. Sing-
ing.

*

Are these words
in or
out of mind?

*

Father coughs
in his sleep, Mother
sighs in hers, nothing
I can do for them.

*

Grow-
ing cold
and old.

*

Raccoons scream
over garbage
and a skunk streams
into my light.

*

Animals quieten
in the center of
dying.

*

In the pane of night
I stare at me
more real than me.

*

Knowing pain
like a difficult
friend.

*

Quaking
I do not
crack.

*

This night
of visionary headache
could not be improved.

*

Milton saw
lights of creation
and judgment
blind.

*

Birds twitter
but
no light.

*

Lightning!
Too late
for truth?

*

How strange.
My life.
No other.

*

The light
of not trying
for light.

*

I could lift
the world off my mind
but where would I rest it?

*

The night is open-mouthed
holding its breath
about to speak
or swallow us.

*

The night is deeper
than darkness
but I see to the end of it.

*

Stars look back
knowing whatever
I see.

*

The sky
my skin
home.

*

Doing nothing
before the fire
fills the night.

*

Moths, and their
dust on the window
words
the dust of their wings.

Moths on the glass
flutter to enter
the mind that thinks they are outside.

*

In mind of night
in the mind of moths
what are they thinking of me?

Thanks for bringing me back
to our glass after wandering—
the glass reflecting me
in your fluttering, dying wings,
reflecting you in these faltering words.

In the dead of night
we suddenly wake to wings
of the sky, and far beyond the sky.

*

Leaves on the window.
Wind from the meadow.
Face leaves the window.

*

The meadow lies
out there, out of mind
minding the strangers of night.

*

Speaking of shadows
of strangers departing
I am on my way.

*

Preparing
for exile
from death.

*

Where am I go-
ing sitting still
so long?
So long!

*

Where are we
if not here?
Not here.

*

The night is so
clear I no
longer look.

*

I have sat so long with the Buddha who is not
and my self that will not go away
that I no longer know which is which.

*

The night is too
quiet for words.
Are only Buddhas
awake?

THE MOON IN MILK

The moon
in milk
hunts for you.

*

Where
is a ray
of your eyes?

*

Who is as bright
as the moon
and as clouded?

*

The moon
hunts hiding
moonstones.

*

The moon
flares meadowstones
back home.

*

Hazed moon
in forbidden trees
we played under anyhow.

*

I go
lost
in glow.

*

Slow moon, I am
yours on the hill of
summers, lasting.

*

A night
I could swim through
to you.

*

The moon
going down
I give up

going.

SEARCHING FOR DAWN

Goldfish
swam as we
slept.

*

Arms going up
hands spreading out
body a flow of slow waves.

*

Searching for dawn
I pad through leaves
to the lake.

*

Light from the lake
leaks through
woods.

*

Reaching
a little more
sky

*

Dew drips
from beached
canoes.

*

I look
at the lake
face to face.

*

That fisherman's
paddling
out of a Chinese painting.

*

Swallows
stitch
lake and sky.

*

Fish rip
the surface
and fall.

*

I dip
my mind
in the water.

*

Does the sun
rise from water
or mind?

*

Sounding the sky
bubbling poetry
through it.

*

Pine boughs
shadow
my poems.

*

A spider
climbs down from my cap
to read my poems.

*

My poems
blow all over
with leaves of Tu Fu and Whitman.

*

Clouds pass
buds
brighten.

*

Weeds
in first light
look good enough to eat.

*

The ease of grow-
ing weeds, the joy
of their perfection.

*

Raindrops
quiver
on the line:
I am thirsty
but only look.

*

The sparrow on the wall
watches me
watching him
watching me fly away.

*

In the garden
squirrels

quarrel.

*

The blue air
bathes
a bluebird.

*

A bluebird's air
bathes
silence.

*

Moss on birches.
Clouds on sky.
Where am I?

*

Stones, moss, dirt
in greenery of light.

*

A garden before gardening:
we have been here all along.

*

Panicking
red
leaves.

*

Beware
be aware
beware.

*

Above all
mind
the birds.

*

Leaves burn
in the sun
like suns.

*

A new
lit
world.

*

Sunshine
melts me
down.

*

Clouds of the mind
drift on.
I touch the sky
with my tongue.

WAVES TELLING THE SAME OLD NOTHING

Waves
telling the same old
nothing.

*

Waves over waves
sound sea-
changes.

*

Churning
white
can't fool me.

*

Storms
on the surface.
Rest in depths.

*

People all gone.
Sand's waiting
for footprints.

*

Who's
drifting from shore
to shore?

*

Who's
deeper
than I?

*

Who touched
all the way
down?

PART II

BREATHING, SWIMMING, SNOWING

I AM HOW I BREATHE

I am how I breathe   beech smoke in rain

leaves eyeing me at dusk   rustling me asleep

eyes harboring a sea

birds swim   fish fly

in tidal green

masts flower   trunks bob

from mossy wrecks

I swim   through fragrant   leaves

laughing

as   I   drown

INCENSE OF SPRING

Incense lingers.
The spark has gone out, ashes
sprinkle your poem.
You have gone away
your smile and everything else.
The air is nearing spring
and I am looking out for you.
The snow is nearly forgotten
graying under the birches.
You are like none of the others
in their separate bodies.
Your incense lingers, your smile
and mind of earth and fire.
I have always known you
in the feel of earth in my hands
fire on my face
and the incense of spring.

THE SEASIDE OF YESTERYEAR

The seaside of yesteryear
is very much with us, still
with its parasols and heat.
The light is steady and free.

On the pier, children run
to the lighthouse and back to the sand
as children are wont to do
but their faces are turned away
and their voices are turned away
so I hear nothing at all
as if sounds had drained away.

You are no longer in sight
not even in shadows of birches
up from the hill, towards lovers
who hid till they passed away
as we have passed away.
I cannot find our bower
nor any sense of you.

Fish lie in murky pools
quiet as Quaker prayers
and a ship waits on the horizon
perfectly bright and still
as if the chronometer stopped
when you slipped over the edge.

O what would bring it all back
your lips and full body of sound?
Listen!—till you feel me
on you embedded in sand
in our heat again.

CRYSTAL SUNLAKE

I walk through smiling heat.
I walk into Crystal Sunlake.
My body stiffens, the chill
stands off from my center.
Smiling I
go under, swim under, stiff
as a waterlogged log, still smiling.

Now I stand on a raft
floating cold in air
staring across Crystal Sunlake
at shore-faces strangely small
until they freeze in view.

You break the ice of the mind
churning the blue towards me.
Diving, my stiff body
shatters the body of water.
We float in watery light.

I walk into the air
blood surging through my body
body surging through air
man I did not know
heavy with watery light
facing your faces in sand
all eyes sun crystals now
seeing one sun one seeing:
nothing more to say.

Always more to say.
We went in less than one
came out many together
turning sounds of water
into the flow of fire:
one body of watery light.

BEYOND LIFELINES

Returning to Pilgrim
woods after city winter
have I been here all along?

June dusk melts old
machinery of snow
that packed the heart
and senses flow
to crickets in sweet grass.

Leaves stir faint light from old summers
old love snowed out from cities.

Still leaves of green flame
gold dust in the air
birds sing more sweetly than choirs of Christians.

Passing the field where we captured the flag
in dusk of Depression and War

I hear Red Rover Come Over
and the King of the Mountain roar

as if I had never left
trees that never grow old:

reunion of boy and man.

*

Heat circles trees and my limbs too.
Leaves fan leaves.
I wipe sweat from my hair.
The gray sky sags.
Something is going to happen:
a change of life?
A storm arising out of
what we have survived?

*

Paring my claws
clenching jaws

tongue digs teeth
instead of telling
hunger and anger

feet sleeping on the cabin floor:
I want to go where?

bay? bridge? ocean? wise
mountains of ancient mist?

I wait for what to move me
out, up, away?

Blood surge? A war?

*

I could have seen the
dawning lake
but I stayed in
afraid

of what? The kettle
steamed. On the porch
I sipped tea.
Why should I be

the first
awake
to dawn
and death?

*

Flames come and go.
Coals glow.
Winds come and go.
Woods sway and stay.
Wherever I've gone
I'm always here
like trees that
feed our fires.

Sighing, drinking
Lapsang Souchong
smoky as woods
burning before me.

Errors burn
to be
free
of my skin.

What's on my mind
but words for silence
beyond the wind?

What's in my heart
but words for stillness
beyond the fire?

*

Returning to my skull
crawling into it to stare
I am body-glow.
This is my body speaking!
I am all about me.
Not the lonely me
that holds itself like gold
a part from an other

O no, no other now
my years flow into yours
I see through your body
you are all about you.

*

Lines of trees
lines of poems
fire of trees
lines of fire
how I glow

paper fish
swim in heat
wanting out
into rain
into clouds

we go

*

All summer, waiting for summer
to hold us forever.
June storms into July
August friends crowding like city
winter, when we waited for woods
and now, in woods, for fall
wanting to stay all year
year after year until
waiting would be forgotten.

*

The dog dozes in the open door
lying belly up with no suspicions

among cornstalks on the porch
where raccoons left them.

Chinese ginger and jasmine tea
summer me back to my body.

My daughter drops dead leaves on me till
I am gratefully dead.

Looking inward
we are about to wake up

to the green glow
of old summers.

Leaves sighing, I am
leaving the cottage of sleep

creeping towards crickets in
leaf mold

scouring rush, shade
of birches bright as whitecaps:

sunshine spilling
through groves of song

blue smoke from cottage
chimneys flowing

across green sways
of leaves

woods breathing me
out and in.

*

Certain our lake is there
dark as love

we
lean

over the dune's warm contours
extend beyond our worldly

limits, our certain
touch of sand and air

and could, with a light lift, soar
everywhere.

*

Saws whine, hammers
hurry cottages up

but no one need
remake me

for doing nothing
is right for now,

I go over
no sumi stroke

just sigh
and pee:

Lao Tzu's
wu wei.

*

Beginning each line
as if finishing my life

moving as endless
waves of light

summering
home in water

swimming beyond lifelines
into clouds.

FIVE FOR THE FIRST AMERICANS

and for Gary Snyder

The Indian graveyard washed away.
For years we stumbled on ribs
and skulls, picking teeth from sand
where storms had washed them down
from bluff roots where they were buried
at some tribe's end of the world
the great lake dying
washing our soles and their bones.

O burn my bones when I'm through!

*

In deer woods, burying Indians'
brown bones gathered from the beach
I enter again dark memories of birth:

mosquitoes over the fungus-path
whining waves of annihilation on my cheeks
shudder me into damp growth of deer woods

where buzzing light flows painfully new
over fresh trillia and ferns
on mounds of trees and graves of Indians.

*

So far I have walked
so far I forgot
what I started for:

from dune roots
to luna leaves
mushroom woods
suicide bluff
beach of bones
sumac farm
meadow stones
between pine woods

in the skin of space
in the breath of time

I wait for the sky
to take me in.

*

On hands and knees
in cemetery wild
strawberries

here I am:
Pilgrim
woods dreamt of in city winters
rooted in graves of Indians
here
wherever I go.

Their sky in my skull.
Clouds pass
leaves darken
glow
I am here and there
breathing their air
walking their earth

one body

rising
raining
burning
storming.

*

Leaving the lake of moons and mushroom woods
tearing my roots from Indian graves and dunes
I'm going back to city masks
muscle-minds and babel storms
off-beats of the heart
battle-swirl and snow of death.

IN WOODS AS DARK AS I

I look at myself as a stranger
looks at a stranger he suspects
of suspecting him of suspicions

watching him enter the woods
at evening and disappear.

Now that I have been looked at
suspiciously I might speak
as if I had something to say
beyond suspicions, smiling,
if I were not lost in the woods.

I am inclined to preach
holier than thou
holier than God
telling everyone off
as if I did not know
I too am lost in the woods

as if they did not know
their glaring imperfections
as if they were not mine
as if I had not
anything to say

that they had not read
somewhere and forgotten
as if I could possibly speak
to anyone but me
outside the midnight woods.

I am inclined to stare
at myself, as if possessed
possessing you in nightmares
as if in love
with nothing but myself

as you, all you, in love
that burns us up, as if
you did not know
you are as nothing as I
in woods as dark as I.

I SEE MY BREATH, THE SNOWING LIGHT

I snowshoed to the brook and back
thumping along in semblance of a poem
wanting to tell my life straight through
but finding no beginning, shape, nor end

wanting to stop wanting
waiting for stopping to come
but woke to a blinding setting sun
where there is nowhere to go.

*

I went out to gaze at stars.
They came bright into me.
I would drift gladly among them:
mind cloud.

Looking for little words
(but they are too big, too loud)
I am tired of people-mind
all the bad dreams of faces.
I am tired of the many
and The One is beyond me, far.

How can I drift
beyond stars?

*

Shoot, shooting star
through my eye:
shoot me to sleep.

*

Sing
whip-poor-will
whip me with your song
awake.

*

I see my breath, the snowing light.
I hear the breathing of my mind.
I do not wait for stepping stones.

I went on too long for light
Streaming from the mouth too far
till my breathing fell apart.

I woke from pieces in a show of light.
My breathing dared to dance again
to songs I watch in snowy air.

NO ONE IS ANYTHING NOW

Birds sang in rainy woods.
Boarded cottages glowed.
In a rush of rain
darkness rose from the earth.
Then the woods went out.
They drip on dead leaves in the dark.

Sounds sink in my throat
as a sailboat sinks in fog.
I lie where we made our first child
who has hitched to San Francisco.
The woods breathe warm and cool
music from the lake through the open
window across my neck
as she dances in strobe lightning.

Rain gentles the roof and stars
the window where firelight strikes it.
Flames come and go and coals
glow on
cold banana soup in a Chinese bowl.
I glow, full of jasmine. Moods
ooze from smoky doze.

I am only an animal whose home is earth.

*

Rain comes and goes.
My head on her painted window throbs
music through dull light.
She has gone, is gone
will be gone tomorrow
with rain on her hair. There she goes
only a child how long ago
now west with him
to swim in seas
at the other end of the earth.

Rainy jungles wait
birds sing in steam
from seas where they will sail.
Where will they build?
In trees where monkeys play?
Mountains where hawks hover?
Beaches where seals sport?
What am I waiting for?

Her rainy voice from the sky.

*

Kneeling by meadow stones
where I stood last winter
alone in the Milky Way

I am not praying, just homing
here like golden lichens
colonizing stones
where a dead farmer loved

my body crawling with bugs
wedding me to weeds
dying into sunlight.

*

Starlight rains on leaves
and my face where I float free
among galactic trees.

Stars snow
in August heat.
We swim over moonlit stones.

*

Starlight snowing leaves
among galactic trees
your face floating free

among moony stones
no wonder I despair
total other there
no wonder, I could float
into the darkening lake.

But knowing you dream of me
knowing we are dreams
there is nothing to hold
nothing of you to cling to.
Memories cloud by.
No one is anything now
but wonder. I float
in a lake of light.

I am swimming around you.
You are swimming away
down moonlight to weeds that freeze
your mouth and thighs.
Your cries bubble through moonlight
into stars of wonder.

HUNGRY GHOSTS

Hungry ghosts pray to the earth for solid flesh.
Slipping through shrouds of rain
they know of nothing to gnaw on.
They prey on thinnest air.

Everywhere I turn, they turn
dancers without music
without any form at all.

And yet I imagine them women
I once held, desiring me
as I desire your emptiness.

Moving through rain
straight as your midnight hair
I stay dry
as dust of leaves or dying cough
praying to the earth for solid flesh.

THREE SNOW SONGS

Snow dusk she
winds yarn
the wind sleeps in
the leaning barn.

*

Snow castle, the moon
over spiky woods
garden black, horses
steaming in the barn
the song goes on.

*

Sing song darkening
walls of fern

for falling sunlight
drowses the eye

and the cup falters
in mossy fingers

all over, all over
the singing closes.

MOON BONES

Trudging in drifts behind our summer-house, I blinked at pines on the hill. They withered beyond my bleached-out world as the moon blossomed in my arms.

*

How could they sleep, the Somonour
and Wif of Bathe and all
before their pilgrimage?
Dreams of final grace
and worldly joys on the way
to the holy blissful martyr
kept their eyes open.

Mine look within.
I have never craved
shrines and relics
because my head is filled
with fetishes of bone
cannibal hair, fire
of generation, mockeries of
reverence my father
taught me

I heard
his piety boom and toll
from pulpits till I glimpsed
a muse in green woods.

Still
I love her more than thunderous
commandments could move me.
The woods have darkened
with his faithful eyes
trees shriveling
with his voice and neck
as I am shriveling too.

Fantasies of green
touches in moonlight
darken snow. How can I
sleep before my pilgrimage
to find her
before the woods are cut?

Will dreams of love
drown me
dragging me down
seaweed-choked
eyes swallowing
oceanic wonders
at the instant of
death?

*

Returning to woods in winter
pilgrim to Pilgrim searching
for the birches where I dreamed
in August sweat and shadow
before fighting in cities
of sterilizing light

   snowy holy
I will find her
   snowy holy

*

Is this the grove where she lay
warm before wars
numbered us nameless?

Is she the moon in the birches
or one of their weaving shadows?
I dance around them
singing in circles
to turn them green

so she will fall like fresh fruit.
I creep but no one comes.

I leap but no one comes.
I push over dead trees to keep
warm. But first
I bow to their shadows
groaning in moonlight. They
fall in shrouds of snow. I tire
quickly of seeming heroic.

Cracking branches I try
to kindle a companion.
Smoke tickles the moon
and my throat. I cough.
No love-death comes for me.

*

Where have ebb and flow
of great lakes gone?
Can songs melt snow
make flowers grow
and bodies join?

*

Shall I wed a tree
like the Roman Frazer described
who embraced her and kissed her
and offered her wine?

My lips freeze
to the bark and tear
I dance round the shining birch
wailing prayers to turn it green.
I climb up to kiss the moon.
Icy fingers of light
close my lids.
Fool!—to fool with the moon:
Moon-fool!

The moon is only a moon.

*

Climbing down
I see footprints leading
out of the grove to bluffs
of love in summers
before one war or another.
Bones lie scattered in snow.
Are they her bones or mine?
I fall on them to trap
whatever memory made them.
Snow flies up like frightened
gulls, beating my face. I run.

*

I climb a dune storm-hollowed
bone-picking a bush.
In it a rusty skull
waits for birth.
Snow-eyed, I ease it out.
I lay it on bones to see
if I can kindle a
companion, warming
her awake. I
light a fire
to love them alive.
Smoke feathers
a face. They grow
flesh of smoke
snowy holy.

Light cascades around us
eyes swallow oceanic wonders
warm tides sway us, we
swim in eternal summer.

THREE FOR THE MOON

Bright mountains at the
black
edge
of the moon

stars
staring into my eyes
coldly burning away
cosmologies

wisps
of galaxies in the glass
whirling the mind away
through my raw
animal
eye

paranoia
of Northern Lights
Venus
blinding

and mindless
dawn.

*

Moon
breath
lights
the river
we
swim
starward

home.

*

The moon
in the pool
where I look for
your face

is the face
behind all masks
wisemen have faced
in scripture or sky

overseeing the dark
mind of vast affection.

PART III

SHADOWS OF BUDDHALAND

WAITING FOR LAO TZU

A woman in me waits
as valleys wait
for rain.

She waits
for a lover
to drown her.

She waits
for a child
to swim from her.

Quietly
she lies
ever giving.

Possessions
pass
away.

The powerful never find her:
dark woman of the valley

hidden deep within us
far from manly
power.

Wait
as she waits
for rain.

A CHINESE TEAPOT

Left on my desk
as if by chance

the teapot was studied:
the cup as if studied

was left beside it
wholly by chance.

*

My fingers moving
as if they are thinking

or as if words are
thinking of themselves

but not self-centered, really
after all, they know

themselves as movement
of hand, man, kind of everything.

*

Nothing moves hands
into a poem.

"I" do not make
the good ones

though I try
like a judge condemning

men he'd reform
to death.

*

When you stare at words
they gape like fish on a pier.

Like fish by a pier
poems hide among rocks.

Among rocks they float
like seaweed in our dreams.

LOOKING FOR MY FACE

Looking for my face
floating in the sea

among ripples of desire
on the verge of sleep

slowly being remembered
in the ebb and flow

looking into waves within
for the face before I was born.

*

Passing through Chinese mountains
at times on a bird, at times
on foot, behind ox-carts and warriors
stumbling through the night

I sit on a skull to write
this poem in peace, alone
where blossoms survive battle
others leaving me

under the moon rising
from waves behind dark hills
moon of my smile rising
from the face before I was born.

ZAZEN AT MYOSHINJI

One smiles, looking down.
One looks up through glasses.
One looks around.
One stares under eyebrows.
One lifts one.
One gazes over hands.
One glances.
One dozes.
One looks at one.
One looks at no one.
One looks as if trying to shit.
One looks as if trying not to.
One looks as if she knows.
One looks as if nobody knows.
One looks as if nowhere.
One looks as if looking.
One looks as if looking at nothing.

YEARS OF CROSSING MY LEGS

After years of crossing my legs, what
do I know of nothing
that I did not know
when I thought I knew
how to cross over
from the way of the cross
to the way of no way?
No way!

SHRINE BEDROOM

Waiting for waking in your shrine bedroom
I sit tight in the sun between traffic and solitude
between my self and yours
just as if, not being—
dozing my way nowhere
a toad in the sun.

Cars jabber mantras of passage
to those whose ears are open.
I am yawning.

The sun spreads light to those whose eyes are open.
It tickles mine wet. I blink
as if under water
swimming up for clarity.

Blinking, I dry them out
squeeze them free of glare
till I see how I am not and say
a breath in a timeless silence.

MATSUI KEIKO

"Pine-well good-child"
wed me in Heian
reflecting the sun
of Goddess and Buddha.

*

With tweezers you bought when we married
on the other side of the world
you pluck lashes growing inward
from the world into your mind

and laugh

watching my eyes watching yours
in the mirror my mother held
before her face when I
strained in her for the world, and you.

*

Lonely? Your friends are as numberless
as grains of genmai
baby carrots you sing to
nori saved from darkest depths
onions you liberated from insects
potatoes eyeing your dancing fingers
daikon longer than your arm
mochi swelling like Hotei's stomach
noodles swimming in your vision.

Each pea and lentil is your companion
enjoying your Zen jokes
your prayers to Buddhas of
soil and air, water and fire
your mantras against polluting demons.

How can you ever be lonely
wherever you wander
to the ends of the earth
your only home?

HOW THE SUN-GODDESS ROSE FROM ISE BAY AND SANK IN LAKE MICHIGAN

After our wedding we
arrived at dusk at an inn on Ise Bay.
Water seeped into the sky
and the sky into our sleepiness
as rain had come and gone and come again.
Or were we underwater in our room
as fish dozed on the table?
Steamy from soup and tea
we came up for air
to play bamboo flutes
but even the tune was soggy.
So we crawled under quilts.

I dreamed that volcanoes of flesh and blood
rumbled together, rose
through the churning sea
to bloom as islands of Japan.

Before dawn I touched your sleeping face
whispering to see the dawn.
But you swam in sea-dreams far below.

Alone, I walked on
the sea-wall in the spray.
The Wedded Rocks, roped
together, rose
from dark waves as I had dreamed
we had emerged from ancient depths.
And as I held my breath, the sun
bled into the waves.

Old men in white robes bowed
clapping to the rising sun
that spilled the blood of all
the dead into the sea
and across the stones at my feet.
I shriveled in the spray
terrified of holiness
dissolving me in the sea.

An old man clopped towards me
on wooden clogs
pulled tight his robe against the light
and smiled to me as I bowed to him
and to his aureoled balding head.
We clapped
to the goddess sun.

Blinded by her bloody glow
of love-light pouring through the waves
I lost him, lost all
human sense
gasping in her light.
As vision cleared to sight
I wiped my eyes free of the
mist of myth. The old man hobbled away.
I hurried back to the inn
before the sun could consume
all she had created and we had spoiled.

*

When the earth had turned to the other side of the sun
she sank in Lake Michigan
as we sat, hands joined,
on the beach near the cross
where Father Marquette
carried ashore by Indians had sighed
"Here I shall finish my voyage."

The sun was only the sun to him
sinking as he sank from the world
to rise to his only God.
My father, another Reverend
half-way to heaven above the beach
watched from a hospital window
the sun set
taking the world's blood with her
to sleep underwater
till she rose again from Ise Bay
as Jesus rose from flesh to heaven.

The Sun and Son join like Wedded Rocks
and all their followers, east and west
north and south
receive their double light till they are one
in love of all the colors
as we are one on body's earth
in mind of sky.

CHRIST AND BUDDHAS IN PILGRIM

In our Pilgrim cottage
twigs hiss in frail flames.
Smoke hesitates. Steam
hovers over teacups.
Hunching, I poke
papers, blow
them ablaze
add logs
living their bright death.

We drink Kyoto tea
under bronze Kannon
who pours a stream of compassion
over the wishing jewel.
On the left, Shakyamuni sits
under the Bo tree, growing
out of it, out of mind.

On the right, Yakushi Nyorai
Buddha-physician of souls
holds out the medicine pot.
On the cross, the Savior's soul
rising from ripped flesh
embraces the fallen world.

I turned away from the cross.
I flew to Buddhas of Japan.
They dissolved in me, as me
till I was nothing but pain
no less yours than mine.
Your empty heart-mind smiled
when my way was lost.

Where there was nothing
love recreated us
on the other side of the world—
pilgrims to this home
drinking Kyoto tea.

HEARING HIM DRONE IN JAPANESE

Hearing him drone in Japanese
circling drunk on mono-no-aware
kimono sleeves flapping in the autumn breeze
she reminisces of hair
when hers was long, never cut
heavy from the bath
a damp burden on her back
hearing him drone of scholars
she reaches backwards through the night
tunneling to midsummer of naked dancing
in the meadow, in the moonlight
in a mild breeze
she could have sunk
into tall grass
drowned in its green swirls
she could have returned to primeval dusk
by simply falling apart
legs sinking, arms melting
breasts bubbling over
the rim of midnight
into the dark beginning of another day
when she would ready herself for
the made up morning
to teach the lies of traffic.

IN THE WISTERIA GARDEN

In the wisteria garden
the Buddhas are waiting for tea.
Are the ladies in kimono
smiling at the Buddhas
or the heady scent of wisteria—
the folly of wisdom or beauty?

The ladies smile as if they are also Buddhas.
Odor of wisteria, taste of tea
confuse all sentient beings
till samsara is nirvana
as it always is.

The Buddhas wait ladylike
as the ladies smile Buddhalike
as is, pouring tea.

LOSING OUR FACULTIES IN JAPAN

A professor of German
crawls for a cup of tea
and back to his seat.

A professor of French
pinches precise pronunciation
from his upper lip.

A professor of English
leans over his notes
as if about to throw up.

Three more professors of English
chins in hands
elbows on table
close their eyes
as if recalling
what Hamlet said
to his father's ghost.

The professor of Russian
peers over his glasses
as he pulls his left ear.
He does most of the talking
when he isn't sniffing.

The only woman professor
giggles at all the speeches.

The fattest briefcase
fools no one.
Nor do the silk suits and ties.

Leaves fall
outside curricula.

The jaws of the lone foreigner
clench as if tetanus
had struck
as he writes:

"Are the teacups
half-full
or half-empty?
Are our minds?"

GOING GOING GOING GONE

A dissonance between us
in love-music between us
as I tell you my hurt in the pasture.

The hurt in my head passes
after wild asparagus
and tea.

You hear and cry with me
holding and letting go.

And when we part
you are a part of me.

My throat and face
open. High calm.

*

The night is curtained out:
all but the crickets' singing.

History is out there too:
all but my hunger

for the past to come into the light
but everyone I love is out, out:

nothing here but me
surely going out.

*

Crows squall over desolate gray
rice fields after harvest.

I wake up cold
blinking away the blur

of years I planned
lying soggy:

no punishment but neglect:
memory of earnestness, a joke.

Van Gogh heard caw-
ing in a sweltering field:

nothing but art then,
nothing now but this.

*

Dry as leaves
that scrape the roof
in the summer night
I call you, wherever you are.

Tired of pushing
useless without you
smoky all over
I want to give up the ghost.

But crickets go on, moths and
flies in the corner keep at it
and the white belly of a tree frog
on my black window twitches
never giving up.

Air cools my face
as if you are breathing the night
nearing
as if I am breathing your breath.

*

A tea-stained empty cup
sits on a shadowed saucer.
The sleek white teapot

points its spout at me.
My tongue-tip twinges
a cavity.

Alone with the dog
lying between irises and muddy boots
I stare at myself
in the grandfather pendulum
that swings before the dignity of pussy willows.

In the sunny air of the farmhouse
in the desperate smell of scrambled eggs
waves of ancient orgasms
sweep me from dead lovers.

*

Cotton, leather, wool
and sadistic words
caress us with total
protection from air
and earth
those honest lovers.

*

Hiking to the forest
I am still in my body
still, with respect to my body
still, respecting my body
we move across the pasture
one, with respect to the pasture
one, respecting the pasture
and sky
one us, pasture and sky.

*

Sitting on a stump by County Z
reading the Tao is like a lifeless crooked tree
I look up at one at the crossroads
of A and Z, the universe's center
where I stood last night under the turning stars
until I saw nothing at all.

*

The last cloud drifted from the sky,
the sun set, the moon set
stars dissolved in
total nothing that would be
clear as dawn if words
O if words stayed away.

*

All has been said of Nothing.
Enough of silence and Void!
They laugh at all said about them
here in the noise of plenty.
The Void is an open mouth.
The Buddha sings fully of
Emptiness:
that is all that's left.

*

This room shines in the house.
The house gleams in the yard.
The yard radiates in the neighborhood of strangers.
Here goes nothing.

This a mood of that:
a toy, blood, a cloud.
How I played all day!
Never saw a plot.

Each begins and flows to its end.
Each is part of all that flows.
Each is ripples in the endless brook.

*

Bluejay bluejay bluejay bluejay:
four bluejays squawking in my tree?
Or is it but one bluejay tree?

*

Spring. Snowing. What's new?
I am telling you green
in green, all green
but no: a lie.

No one hears me anyhow.
No one knows how dead
the world is here.
The only life is snow
except for this poor
excuse for me, my breath,
and words: semblances of
life.

So on I go in green
makebelieve, till
telling spring is true.
Till then, what's new?
Spring. Snow. What's new
at noon of make-believe?

I'm still traveling
here at home:

going, going, going, gone.

A MORNING OF NOTHING TO DO

Waking
from busy
bodies

to vast
sky
light.

*

The infinite fades fast
skyblue firming up
in a cracked ceiling
above this lumpish body
mummied by bright quilts.

I am darkly in my mind
nose sticking out of quilts
chilled in walled-in air
sniffing to stay alive
snuffling for food or sex
or any finite joy
imagined in my belly
that rumbles into tune.

*

Kissing fish
glance at me and pass on
wall-eyes like shooting stars
their tight lips craving each other.

The hunger!—crawls in my belly
and in dark seas where I
prehuman, swam
ignorant of land
in awful depths
of ravenous mouths.

Hunger
for sky
light!

*

Is this a museum of death?
(What museum is not?)
Under the paralyzed clock
under the headsman's axe
and cabinetted skulls
in front of mummied freaks
am I an artifact
waiting for public eyes
to wake me into a dance?

*

A morning of nothing to do.
Air sighs slightly beyond
motionless flowery curtains.
The floor shines, clear of people.
The chairs have never been emptier
and the clock stopped ages ago
before the staring fish
were invented for the awakening.

I too have stopped
propped up for mourners.
But there is nothing to mourn
no one to die or be born
in the fish's eye
in this frozen room
in this morning of nothing to do.

*

Hearing you scuffling below
I imagine you squinting
under your hooding lids
waiting for the one
real image
snapped.

Then plunging negatives into
the dialectical soup
developing blacks and whites
celluloid yin and yang
and fixing though nothing is fixed
for me, not even my blanketted body
is fixed as your image is fixed.

So I have begun these poems
to fix an image or two:
mummied life in death
poet wrapped in quilted words.

*

Where does my body end?
In a touch of quilt or guilt
of cold air on my nose?
In the blue of walls
or wakening glass
or in sky light or galaxies
computed by future bodies
of my blood?
If my body is all that may be
in any words imagined
is it more than nothing at all?

From Pacific to Atlantic I stay put
in my familiar body universe.
Spring has turned to winter on it, but
the changes have changed.
Cold air clings to my nose.

I stay.
The rest goes on, all but my rest, it stays.
Homeless, I belong
in this body home
in this loafing art
in this morning of nothing to do.

A SNAPSHOT OF ALLEN GINSBERG

Slipping into a mudra on the sidewalk
giving the Other the finger
grinning around the outbreath
starry teeth staring out of your skull
above its shrunken brother
hanging from your neck
watch ticking lies of samsara
among beads on a string of non-being
outbreathing a funny smile
of one nonentity to another.

GINSBERG EMBRACES FATHER MARQUETTE

(for Allen Ginsberg's reading at the University of Wisconsin—
Milwaukee in 1967 after Marquette University had banned him)

A day will come when Ginsberg and Father Marquette
  embrace on a snowy Wisconsin shore
and in the Joan of Arc Chapel
  Menominees will chew peyote with Joan
    hallucinating immortalizing fire
in cathedrals all over the world
  priests will intone Kaddish
    churches imploding like light bulbs
    corporations tumbling
    multiversities crumbling
    governments and old generals fading away

the Pope dancing with Krishna
Mao chanting with Buddha
LBJ composing interminable illuminated elegies
  to Vietnamese dead
the wolf lying down with the child amputee
  to lick her wounds
the human race will be run
Blake returning in the "human form divine."

On that day all hearts will beat underground
  in volcanoes of affection
hair growing all over the globe
  in a jungle of Eden
    where everyone naked as eucalyptus
      make love, their voices winging
        through entanglements of flesh.

WHY MY POEMS AND I ARE NONZEN

Well,
I no longer practice zazen
nor obsessively read Dharma in English
nor strain my brain on koan
nor practice haiku, calligraphy, ikebana, karate,
Noh acting, action painting, aliotic music
nor paint my room black, windows, toilet, mirrors also
a deep black on black for emptiness
beyond words or images
nor duel with invincible swordsmen climbing
        Red Fuji indifferent to victory and death
nor shoot arrows from a white horse galloping on
a bloodsoaked beach outnumbered 1000 to 1
nor sit in silent seppuku with a short sword
slicing my belly
calmly watching my guts spill out
as my best friend slices off my head
nor in a lone cockpit crash a Zero into
an American aircraft carrier
shouting Banzai in the explosion
as Emperor Hirohito broadcasts surrender
nor oneup a roshi with a slap on the face

nor practice Beat Zen penetrating
every orifice within reach
dead or alive
with my holy ding-dong
while hitching to San Francisco or Denver
high on LSD, Tequila, AND medical maryjane
nor teach spontaneous bop poetry AND prose
        at Naropa Institute
nor practice the Zen of Wall Street OR PR.

But don't get me wrong, no way!
I love Shakyamuni, Bodhidharma,

Han Shan, Daisetz Suzuki, Masao Abe,
Allen Ginsberg, Gary Snyder, Tofu Roshi,
Thich Nhat Hanh AND Ghost Dog,
The Fourteen Dalai Lama,
Mr. Miyagi AND the Karate Kid,
not to mention others of their ilk

AND the androgynous Kannon,
Aung San Suu Kyi
and all those anonymous women
wise, compassionate, strong, and free.

FIRST WORDS OF SUMMER

At last! First words
of summer

after forgetting how poetry
long lies in wait
to spring at our throats.

And the poet?
He whose speech is musical;
she whose dance is spoken;
he whose touch rings true;
she whose taste illumines;
he whose vision harmonizes
her mental body with the world.

Speaking as a poet
I am not myself.
Who was I
when I was I?
And where
when I was not
among the stars?

Not the stars
of a summer night
not even stars telescoped
to the earthy eye

but galaxies of thought
created, swirling me
up and away
through black holes
worm-holes
holiness

destroyed
with a snap
leaving this non-I
in no-space:

poetry
at last!

STAYING IN THE BROOK

The brook
sings
over stones.

They stay put
waiting for me
to sit.

And so I sit
on one and wait
for stars to turn.

Trees turn
air is turning cool
summer turns away—

all changing
but stones
in the cold

curling
undertow
of singing:

the way
I stay
a stone.

PART IV

I-THOU POEM FOR KENNETH REXROTH'S CENTENARY

The numbers in parenthesis refer to pages in *The Complete Poems of Kenneth Rexroth*, edited by Sam Hamill and Bradford Morrow, Copper Canyon Press, 2003.

University of Chicago
Students let me be
With your *Complete Poems*
On a dim lit sofa in International House.
You haunt this Gothic campus
As you did in adolescence
Discovering your genius
In classics without matriculating.
You began a lifetime of rewriting
Japanese, Chinese, Greek,
Latin, and French poems
In American English
As if you were each poet-
Ono-no-Komachi,
Li Po, Sappho,
Abelard, Lorca,
Reverdy, among others

Living though long dead—
Living now in the now
That was their ancient now.
You read, wrote, lived poetry
Among your cubist paintings and
Anarchist polemics
Rousing Chicago rabble
From Wobbly soapboxes
To be themselves
With others
To free themselves
With others
In Bughouse Square
In the Windy City on the make
By the lake.

Reading your lyrics of love in Jackson Park
I remember cycling Saturdays
To its Japanese garden and folk village
To the cool barn of a temple where I first
Read your poems, sipping
My first green tea in the peaceful dark
My first taste of Japan
Before it visited Pearl Harbor.

Now you creep in the shadows
Of this classical library
Returning as you return
To me often since your death—
Not one of those "modest angels
... with never a question
Of the 'ineluctable modality'
Of the invisible" but
Like a sage from Hades;
Or horny Einstein, wandering
Among "coal pockets
In the galaxy, dark nebulae,
And black broken windows into space"; (25)

Or Chuang Tzu floating in the Tao.
You are creeping towards me
Like an ancient turtle
From whose cracked shell
The Chinese told the future
Before you told it in poetry
Of prophetic vision
"Of the fall of history
And waste of fact..." (240)

Your cloudy lids, heavy with dreams
Suffused by memories of lustful love
And loving lust,
Glow from art, poetry, philosophy,
Scarred by fact. Your body is
Bloated with aches of lost love
And immortalized slaughter of
Revolutionaries.

You have come again
From beyond the mountains
Just when I need you, as always,
As this poem gnaws on my mind
Gradually, word by word,
In my aging mind.
You always return when I hear you in your poems.
Welcome back. Sit beside me.
Sink into that cushion.
I was remembering the temple in Jackson Park,
Your words, your mournful voice...
"Chill and abandoned, the pavilion
In Jackson Park stands like a sightless
Lighthouse beside the lake." (68)
You croak like you had swallowed
Basho's frog. You always growled and grumbled
Even when happy. You
Muttered when you weren't shouting.
A mutual friend who read

Every word of yours he could find
Switched off Pacifica Radio
To choke your deathly voice.
It stopped days before your death.
Helpless in bed, you looked, you saw,
You squeezed my hand
But could say nothing
Just as now, profoundly silent
Suffused by remembered speech,
You slouch like a clumsy Buddha.

I'm always glad you return, despite my gripes.
I never know if you know what I'm thinking.
Your face is an enigma, like your cubist poems,
Your wrinkles like those fragments of mad passion.
One advantage of the living over the dead:
I glimpse your creative mind
As your poems pass through mine.
In mine are words from yours
In rhythms of your breathing
Passions of your body
In this world we meet in
even now.

You have come very far
From your favorite constellation:
"'There's Orion!'
The most beautiful object
Either of us will ever
Know in the world or in this life..." (537)
You said to your daughter
Holding her hand one Christmas Eve
In San Francisco long ago
As if it were today
In a poem that takes us there:
"A Sword in a Cloud of Light."
I read it to my daughters every Christmas.
Your stars are now your home.

You must be far colder there
Than on snowy mountains
And silently alone
Far from the warring world;
Why do you return?
Did you stop in Santa Barbara
At your tomb above the Pacific—
A fleeting thought in Buddha-mind,
And in my mundane mind.

You sniff and smile, so I'll go on:
Why do you return?
When you were most alive,
Loved and hated by many
Why did you call and write
This provincial anarcho-
Pacifist
professor/poet
For twenty years, and
Tell me whenever we met
Your troubles, doubts, ideas
When I could only stare, helpless
Trying to make sense of
Everything you wrote and said
And the warring world
You illumine?

I struggled to discover
All of your ideas
Cohering in one
Vision radiating in poetry
As "actual speech of person to person,"
"Communication raised to the highest power,"
"Communal sacrament":
How craft is vision and vision craft;
How communication, communing, and community
Inseparably interdepend. (*Revolutionary Rexroth*)
Unique among modern poets

You are rational and mad
Logical and wise
Philosophical and visionary
As a hooting owl in peopleless woods
At midnight, moonless
As a dreaming corpse.

You were not my guru,
Not on your life or death.
I never worshipped you
Or justified your faults.
You were my mentor, muse
As Yosano Akiko was yours
As Marichiko.
I merely wrote you into books of prose,
Mere prose excepting one small poem
Before this poem
That we are inside now:
"Rexroth crept out
On stage
Heavy, slow to speak
Like an ancient tortoise
From whose calligraphic shell
The Chinese told the future."

Am I your Thou or you my I?
As years passed, coherence cracked,
Splintered,
Your life, your work fragmented
Into contradictions.
In visionary enigmas
Whatever happened to our reason in Japan?
About philosophizing
(Yours? Mine? Any abstractions?)
You quietly wrote
Reminding us,
"How comfortable, and how verbal." (243)

"Trouble is," you once told me,
"You never tell me I'm full of shit!"
I sometimes thought of it
After you pontificated
Denouncing this or that
For flaws that seemed too human
To be inexcusable
But I was much too awed
By your eloquent charisma
To complain
Until it was too late,
The context lost forever.
I was afraid of losing you,
My closest friend, the deepest,
And most troublesome.

But now that you are
Just a thought in Buddhamind
I must confess
I'd rather read the phonebook
Than your cubist poems.
And I thought it strange
That such an inspiring anarchist
Could be almost as patriarchal
As the Pope.
I never thought I'd say it.
But how could you be an anarchistic Catholic?
How can you smile like that?
Shall I go on being honest for a change?
You were the angriest Buddhist since Nichiren
Furiously lashing those blinder than yourself
Or just ignoring you,
The most promiscuous advocate of
Feminism AND "holy matrimony"—
Your home-brewed brands of them.
You egoistic advocate of
Christian self-sacrifice and Buddhist self-negation!

I thought that would get your goat
But you're laughing without a sound
Your distended belly
Bouncing on the sofa
—Full of it?—
Is that the challenge
You wanted to hear?

So I'll go on.
During bloody clashes of
Your comrades and oppressors far below
The mountains you were climbing
How could you create elegies
Of destruction of the People
Art, and Nature
Between spasms of visionary love?

Remembering
The greatest revolutionary poem I know
With the unpronounceable title
Never collected till after you died—
"Noretorp-Noretsyh." (18)
You envision anarchist martyrs
Charging against the Red Army
As it slaughters Hungarians in 1956
While in Golden Gate Park
You lust after glorious thighs
On the bicycle ahead of your own.
Why weren't you ever martyred?
Oh, I didn't mean it that way,
The awful way it sounds:
I've never wished you martyred
For others' liberation.
I don't doubt your courage
Writing what you said,
living what you thought.
But how did you survive

Sticking your neck into the
Dialectical guillotine
To denounce the executioners
And live to tell the tale
Laughing all the way home
To 230 Scott Street
Just in time for the Anarchist Circle
To be seated in your library
Feeling the birthpangs
Of the San Francisco Poetry
Renaissance
And the long overdue
Counterculture.

How could you survive
One counterrevolution after
Another, ideals betrayed
By idealists and cynics alike?

How could you remain
Not just alive but perpetually
Creative while
Those poets you mourn
In "Thou Shalt Not Kill"
Risking less than you
"Stopped writing at thirty?"
"How many are lost in the back wards
Of provincial madhouses?"
Or killed themselves instead of others?
You meant more than all of them
Even when struck mute.

You have won the right
To close your eyes
Sink into that sofa
Letting your poetry
Speak for itself in our memories,

Immortalizing those sacrificed
For liberty, the beauty of art and women,
Love of nature and one another,
Those struggles had to fail
Before you saw the light
The tragic light that Shakyamuni,
Sophocles, and Jesus saw.
You lived to tell the lives and deaths
In "The waste of history..."
To keep alive ideas and
In death to make us more alive
Than we have ever been.

"This is the minimum negative
Condition, the 'Condition humaine,'
The tragic loss of value into
Barren novelty, the condition
Of salvation, out of this alone
The person emerges as complete
Responsible act—this lost
And that conserved—the appalling
Decision of the verb 'to be'." (269)

Making love in the mountains
In your tragic poems
Immortalized those liberating heroes
In your wHoly responsible act.
I remember you in Kyoto
Where you wanted to die
Before crossing the Pacific
To Calfornia.
You were sitting among the Buddhas
Far off from your books and mountains—
In empty light within
The fulsome void.

Once when I read you you were wise.
Next when I read you you were mad.
And now when I read you you are dead.
And what am I
What are you
But I-Thou
Now, forever?
You vanish, but your words remain
Distilled from the *Manyoshu*:
"Weary of the twin seas of
Being and Non-being, I
Long for the mountain of bliss
Untouched by the changing tides." (664)

ABOUT THE POET

MORGAN GIBSON, born June 6, 1929, is a poet, scholar, critic, and prose-writer who won a *Mutiny* Fiction First Award for "Nice Work If" and an Outstanding Scholarly Book Award from *Choice* library journal for his *Revolutionary Rexroth: Poet of East-West Wisdom*. His work has been published in Japan, England, Canada, Switzerland, Thailand, and Italy, as well as the USA, and some has been translated into Japanese, French, and Italian. He has given many readings and lectures in the USA and Japan, where he taught in universities in each country for twenty years. For his next book he is editing his countercultural prose and "Madam CIA," a doggerel Brechtian farce performed by the Demilitarized Zone Troup at anti-war demonstrations. He has a BA from Oberlin College and an MA and PhD from the State University of Iowa, where he participated in poetry writing workshops taught by Robert Lowell, Karl Shapiro, and Paul Engle. His archives are in the University of Chicago Regenstein Library.